ALL IS IN A DREAM

ALL IS IN A DREAM

By Nathan Charles Sollish

Published by
Midnight Express Books

ALL IS IN A DREAM

Copyright © 2013 by Nathan Charles Sollish

ISBN-10: 0990318346

ISBN-13: 978-0-9903183-4-7

Cover art by Jason Weiesnbach

Published by

Midnight Express Books
POBox 69
Berryville AR 72616
(870) 210-3772
MEBooks1@yahoo.com
http://www.MidnightExpressBooks.com

ALL IN A DREAM

By Nathan Charles Sollish

This is an Act . . .

let your mind be the Play.

Act 1

Ah, 'twas a *twinkle* of sound,

as the *raspberries* fell *so short* to the *ground.*

And oh, when I looked out *into the sea,*

I could *feel the whole* world, *melt about me.*

As *wandering along,* I *came* to a *tree,*

that *proved* to me, nature really WAS me.

It *leafed* me *alone,*

as I *plotted my course,*

and *blocked* out my *sound,*

as to *make my throat hoarse.*

And *soon* I was nothing,

lying *flat* on the ground,

as my *dog and cat* quivered,

1

to a *god awful sound.*

And a *flame came from nowhere,*

and it *left me alone,*

with *some* things left *burning,*

and *that god awful* tone.

It *wanted* me *to listen,* to separate *life;*

and *created* a vision of a world with no strife.

And this *tone* took my worries, and drove them away,

but that *god awful sound,* is *still here today.*

I *wanted* to *lose* it, as a child about *three,*

but I found I was *crazy,* if I *took* it from me.

So I *learned* to live WITH it, as I traveled *along,*

and all it would be was a *beautiful* song.

(*Then* was a time, that *WASN'T* so nice,

when I walked with a *lady,* in *hopes* for some rice.)

That *tone* would say SOMETHING,

and it *seemed she could Hear,*

"Believe in God, *child,* and *throw away* FEAR!"*

So *believe me,* I *TELL* you, as I put *down* my foot,

that a sound, DEEP WITHIN, isn't ALWAYS understood.

'Cause it *told me to sit down,*

and *gather up life,*

and *separate love songs,*

and separate strife.

And it told me no *worldly* thing, *ever* will do,

And to top *that* one off, it said, *pass* it to you.

I *think* all my friends, would all pass on new ways,

If I *ever* did tell of my *earlier* days.

The ones when for one man, the ladies were four,

And not a one could you dare call a whore.

So petite and gentle, so frail and discreet,

and I sang with them softly, as they wet down my feet.

Yes, the lasses would mingle, as the men talked their game,

And the ladies would whistle, if a man's legs looked lame.

And a wide sky of beauty would fill my life well,

As I started to see Heaven, and could tell it from Hell.

I started to see Heaven and could TELL it from Hell,

Now *that* is a thought, *I* remember so well.

Ah, but a *whisper*, as I pass this to you,

With the *deepest* of feelings, in *hopes* to get through.

And I *pass* you a *blessing*, God sent you, through me.

Now, you *might* think it selfish, but it *didn't* come *free*.

It started from   a *whisper*, that said, "*I* am the *Light*,"

And it told me, "LOOK INWARD," and *you'll* be all right."

And so, my journey *took* me, from the *World's* wrong and right,

And *instead*, taught me *something*, and it *had* to be L*ight*.

4

(Ah But *not* to forget *visions*, and

Plasticene Thought!

"You can *BE-LIEVE* in *Jesus*,

But don't *buy* what I bought!")

It was an *interesting day*, as I *sat* by the *Tree*,

I found an *old flag*, that was *battered by the sea*.

I laid it *beside* me, in a *most* peculiar way,

And used it for *fun'rel*, as the *preacher* would say.

I *saw* myself lowered, *down into the ground*,

As my *dog and cat quivered*, (to a *god awful sound*.)

I *saw* myself lowered, (*down* into the ground),

(I lay, and said *nothing*, just *wearing a frown*),

In three days of *mourning*, I battered no *eye*,

I *asked* for no *Mercy*, I *wanted* to *die*!

I *saw* the World *dismal*, and so full of *hate*,

That the *name* of the Game, was *Hurry* and Wait.

(There *was* an old *sweeper*, Whose Tale would *Unfold*,

that the *Words* I have *Spoken*, have *Yet* to be Told.)

(And I *told* you *long Time* now, that the *Answer Inside*,

Might bring You to Mercy, *that* your *Love* need not hide.)

Now my Dreams, they all fashion into One

Simple Lace,

That it *fit* 'round her *garter*,

but *worn* 'round her *waist*.

And the *ribbons* were *plentiful*,

all 'bout her hair,

and my *love* did pour *over*,

for to *reach* her, I care.

And my *Children* were Empty of a *Child's* Broken Dream,

And I had to *Chance* it,

just to *See* what I mean.

And my Days were *Outnumbered*, as the *fires* drew *near*,

and my *Mind* screamed "Why me," as if *death* I had *feared*!

So I Ran to a level, as to see the *whole* ground,

And I *called* out to Jesus, *'case HE* was around.

But *No One* would Answer, so *Fate* set my Path,

I had *Come* Here to *Suffer*, and Endure *God's* full Wrath.

And my *Father* had Spoken, that it's *not* what it Seems,

And I had to Forgive *Him*, just to *see* what I mean.

Yes, I had to Forgive *Him*, if the *journey* was near,

For my *father* will Forgive *me*, and remove *Him* one fear.

(Ah, the coffin is *empty*, as I *lie* on the *floor*,

And the *Golden Light through me*, is

now *cast* on the door.)

"I AM NO LONGER *BROKEN*, AS A *CAST-AWAY DREAM*,"

. . .

" I am *Learned*, am *forgiven*, and *do see* what *I mean* . . ."

                     With the Meaning *behind* me,
        and the

forest Ahead,

                     What could One want *More*, than
        to *be*

Better off dead.

As the Sky *does* creep onward, and *this*

Rock does soar on,

(I could *take* you to Heaven, just to *sit on the lawn*.)

I could *take* you to *Heaven*, just to *see*

what I mean,

But *that* would *mean nothing*, for it's *Only a Dream*.

And I *Dream fairy-maidens*, Out to *Sea*, (in a boat,)

living   *Dreams* Beyond *Anything*, I *ever* wrote!

(I *confess*, in my *dreams*, there is *also* Desire,

to go *find* those ladies, and *see* them for hire.

To go find a *Judge and a jury*, (or so,)

And *sit* them *all* down, telling *them where to go*.)

So the Stars fall to *feed* me,

as I *cross this great plain*,

And I *find* myself *hurried*, (at the

beat of the rain.)

And the thunder, come crashing as the

evening came down,

And the *horrid dream fluttered*,

as my *Sleep* 'came More Sound.

End Act 1

Act 2

Oh, my Words are for *Hearing*, and I *give* Them to ears,

While the *Stupid* do Listen, the *minds* They do *Jeer*.

And the mice of misfortune seemed to eat all my

cheese,

when the curfew is over, there's still *never*

a sneeze.

And my father had plenty of *peanuts*

to sell,

so we gave them to Mother, and she

gave us *all* HELL.

And things *seemed* to be HAPPY,

as the evening drew near,

      but the sun was up *early*,

and a new day to fear.

      And I cried out for *mercy*, as my dreams echoed on,

Well I should have been in New Jersey,

where girls have clothes on.

Aw, it don't matter anyhow,

I got what it takes.

(The world calls it hands that *make* no mistakes.)

                Now, I call out to
          whisper the

name of my Soul, and it *tells* me to *silence* my most precious
      goal . .

it tells me to press on, that I may feel good,

but I dwindle, and worry and I CRY (LIKE I SHOULD.)

And I toss, and I turn, as I search for new hope, and

my mind lingers on in its efforts to cope.

And I cry for the seasons to pass with great pride,

as the morning of sunshine casts rays on deers hides.

And I walk 'er so slowly, to the den of my words,

And I place on the table all the things I have heard.

And I memoir a *teacher* that told me to go,

when I reached for her glory, Oh, *ever* so slow,

And my words tried to reach *her*, of the dreams

I once had,

'bout a crew of young maidens, who swam *home* and

were glad.

Some chipper sweet ladies, all bitter with salt,

wet, but still welcome, it was *nobody's* fault.

And I moved over slowly, as I tried now to say,

to my teacher, I love you, and bring a new day.

And I *told* her of waters, that ran through the sand,

and *she* told me, GO now, but take hold ' her hand.

So little was *I* at the offer of *thus*,

that I rambled on *ANYWAY*, *she* started to *cuss* . . . !

 She finally LISTENED, (which is what I had *feared*),

 And she took a picture *of* me, and she drew on a

 beard!

 (She *claimed* it was *peacetime*, but she *worked* for the

war.)

 ' said her *dad* was a commie, and her *mother*, a *whore*.

 And she *gambled* at *nothing*, (although *clean* she was

NOT.)

But her *nickname* was *Mercy*, so you *know* what *she's* got!

And the money she carried, was to *her*, Heaven's Beam,

but I used it to get back to *my*

only dream.

I used it to land in a far-away place, where the

people were PLENTY, and the FOOD a *good* taste.

Where I asked the head butler to show me the room,

and he handed me a bucket, and he handed me a broom.

And my mother was happy there, for she lay down to rest,

all the worries and troubles of *Life's* only Test.

And my *father's* not forgotten, and my *brothers* are

the *same*,

How can I forget *them*, if I can't dodge the *rain*!

HOW can I forget those who *brought* me to earth?

(MY *MOTHER* FORGOT ME AS *SOON* AS SHE *GAVE BIRTH!*)

I try to look on, *past* the ceiling and floor,

as to find and look INTO that *MOST* hidden door.

To find such a prize, and to look in and see,

would be all the reason to finally *Be.*

Would be all the *reason* to sit down and chat

Would be *all* the reason,

(If *that's* where it's AT!)

End of Act 2

Act 3

It could be such a mess, (and would be such a sin),

if I couldn't get back to the Ocean again.

Where those *most* simple maidens, in a *most* simple hush,

could tickle my fancies, and make them *BOTH* blush.

I could sit in the boat, as I'd paddle the way,

as my beautiful crew would set forth a new day.

And one day it HAPPENED, yes,

just as I planned . . . the Ocean was dry, and we rest in the

sand.

And the ladies looked FUNNY, as they *realized* their fate,

as I moved slowly toward them, in my *eyes* they did rate.

And I managed to PUSH them, way out from the sand,

as the sky busted out, with a four piece brass band.

And I screamed "can't you SEE it, it's the *end of all war!*"

But they all seemed to SHOW that they've *seen* it before.

Then a voice came from Heaven, said "ALL TAKE YOUR PLACE!"

and the ladies looked UPWARD, and they threw the sky lace.

Then a set of eyes opened, in the cloud, (as to see),

and a voice said that all of us PRESENT were free.

And the Ocean then LIFTED, and it gave us a tow,

and it showed us our freedom, as to *see* what we Know.

And the ladies all huddled, as I cast a great sail,

from the long johns and laces that we got in the mail.

And we made a great FLAG that produced such a clash,

that the ladies all shed it, and made a great sash.

And we wrapped it 'round Heaven, and we tied it 'round Hell,

just to show all the world, we were *all* doing well.

(I must cling to Sabbath

as to not go to Hell,

If I do get to Heaven,

I will know it *quite* well.

But

if I could *ever* reproduce
rain,

I *still* couldn't witness
Creation

again.)

(I liked to sing SOFTLY, as the ladies did hum),

but a great voice from Heaven, really *made me* feel dumb . . .

It seemed to be *shrieking*, at a *God* awful tone,

and it certainly *made* me feel most all alone.

So I creeped over lasses, and I laid down to rest,

and I knew THAT day, I had done *all* my best.

So I prayed for the children, who were out in the

cold,

and I prayed for them, houses, BEFORE they grow

old.

And I prayed for old ladies and old men to wed,

It's much more enlightening, than lying

'round DEAD.

And I prayed for the rabbits to be more than

stew,

And I prayed for God's Children, which is what

we ALL do.

And I blessed all the paupers, who were *NEVER*

well fed,

then I wrapped up my body, and went off to bed.

And when I awoke, there were ladies *galore,*

but when I looked out, I saw *nowhere* was shore.

SO I looked through the package, that they sent

us from home,

and I wrote me a letter, as to not feel alone.

And I gave it to Prudence, yes the one with

no sense,

and she read it, and ate it, and called it

past tense.

Then she offered me milk, that a lady had flown,

to a land beyond Heaven, that we ALWAYS have known.

And she gave me a bottle, and a note that was PART,

And it said,

"If you READ this, you must
OPEN your heart."

And I glanced a bit downward, (as to see what to see . . .), and I saw two initials, that read *clear* . . ."J.C."

So I drew out a map, as to plot a new

course,

and I screamed for the Captain, 'till my

voice did go hoarse.

Then I realized the ladies were all

fast asleep

(I need a new Captain, this *plot* for

to keep).

As the morning drew closer, I counted my lass,

just to find one was *missing*, and the curse, it was CAST.

I had found one was MISSING, as to seal up my fate,

and begin the worst plight, that I *EVER* did rate.

(I had girls for Sunday, and Monday, and Tue',

but now what of Wednesday, Lord *WHAT* shall I do?

It's a *long way* to Heaven, to be *without* Sue,

It's a LONG way to Heaven, so *what* shall I do)?

As I pondered my *question*, my stomach did groan,

and I yelped out a sound in a GOD-AWFUL moan.

I strained out to SEE if my feelings were right,

and Nancy and Julie *WERE* into the night.

It seemed to be *over*, having three days to fill,

and a voice kept reminding me, "THOU SHALT NOT KILL."

If I had my *dog* with me, I'd have thrown

him a *bone*,

But he *liked* the Green Mountains, so I

left him ALONE.

He liked the Green Mountains, where for

YEARS he has played,

(And he liked them so much, that that's

where he *STAYED*).

End of Act 3

Act 4

Ah, the birds DO soar upward, as my words

                do caress,

a vision of FREEDOM, that I put to God's

                test.

I'm managing to *see* that this dream is

                for REAL,

(It's a matter of knowledge ... or JUST

                how you FEEL).

It's a time to forget ALL, (the things

                of the *past*),

and begin to spend *time* with the things that

                do LAST.

It's a time to rejoice at the world turning COLD,

for the day DOES grow LONGER, and the YOUNG

DO grow old.

And the *money* you're savin',

is as useless as *TRASH*,

So you might as well BURN it, and GIVE UP on

cash.

"You *might* let your *body* caress the sun's beam,

as you might catch ME doing, if you catch my

next Dream ..."

A young maiden asked a question that she tried to unfold,

"Is it Heaven, when I die, or just what I'm

TOLD?

So I told her, "LIE DOWN," (that I'd do her so well),

Well, she WANTED to go to Heaven, but she WOUND UP

in Hell.

She wound up UNWORTHY of God's Only Dream,

and I asked God's forgiveness, so you'll SEE what

I mean.

It's a long night *ahead*, and I'm REALLY low *staffed*,

So I asked God for Mercy, and it seemed the sky laughed.

It seemed that that SOUND had turned to a *drone*,

and it was time once *again* to hear from that tone.

So I THEN closed my eyes, as to THIS world not see,

and I shut off all SOUND, as to let this world BE.

And I looked instead INWARD, just to see what was right,

and I found that the Answer was ONLY God's Light.

And that SOUND raged on LOUDER, as to set a new toll,

and my Eye *was* now open, to see IN at my Goal.

Like a wise man who
TOUCHED me,

like a fire that burned.

I looked DEEPER

inward,

to SEE what I learned.

And I RAN through the
thickets,

as to *find* a new path,

but ONLY to FIND and
ENDURE

God's Full Wrath.

(To *endure* such a Journey would SEEM quite *insane*),

but I WANTED to SEE all God's Children *again*.

I wanted to *lead* them, to show *them* the way,

but instead I found pathways that led FROM that Day.

Yes, instead I found SOMETHING that put up a wall,

but showed me in Heaven, men surely *don't* fall.

Yes, it *showed* me a knocker that just hung from the
door,

and it showed me Disease don't just come from a whore.

It showed me blue ribbons were NICE for a lass,

but what will it DO you, if you don't have the *class*.

It showed me a flower, *without* any dew,

and it *showed* me God's Children, but only a *few*.

It showed me a RICH MAN, who showed me the way,

by leaving it ALL, just to buy a new Day.

(But WHAT GOOD is something that you *don't*

understand,

like a boat full of LASSES, drifting in

towards the sand)?

Now the cloud did draw black, as the blackest

of coal,

as we came near a lily that was floating by all.

And ONE said to *pluck* it, and cook it with rice,

and *another* said to eat it with BARLEY, so nice.

And we *all* watched it drift, in a deepness of blue,

as we *all* tried to figure out just *WHAT* to do.

And as it drifted out, you could no *longer* see

green,

And that lily turned to DAISIES, as it DOES, in

a Dream.

And the birds of FREE THINKING soared *high*

overhead,

as to show all the word that God is *not* dead.

And His Spirit DOES LINGER, as to *watch* a child grow,

and my Father does tell ME to let this world go.

LET THE WORLD FEEL *SEXY*, WITH NO ONE TO SAY
NO!

(I'd rather paint *daisies*, and watch a GOOD SHOW.)

I'd RATHER paint daisies, (if you know what I MEAN),

Because DAISIES are NORMAL, if you live in a Dream.

So to the world I'm NUTS, and I *really* have no Class,

for I choose to float freely, in a boat full of lass.

Yes, I choose to be CAREFUL, as to not press my *luck*,

When I *started* this journey, I *knew* I was stuck.

I strained my Eye inward, as to witness my plight,

but the *harder* I looked, the more I saw Light.

The more I saw *Misery* as man's only choice,

to set with his MONEY, as he drives his Rolls Royce.

Which is *WHY* I wound up here, to *discover* my goal,

and write *you* a message, as the funeral bells toll.

End Act 4

Act 5

The winds came and blew us afar to Madrid,

where we captured a maiden, and her four year

old kid.

And we brought them to Egypt, where they no longer

rest,

for the great SPHINX has called them, to put them

to test.

And clouds turn to satin, as the grains of

sand fly,

from the East to the West, with no troubles

to hide.

And the rain washed my clothing, as a child would

drop food,

(as my mother did TELL me, that a child was quite

rude.)

And my oars were

all broken, and my day was for STOOL,

and my dad said a

broken OAR, was like a broken RULE.

And IF you did break it, you would *see* what I MEAN,

you would drift on FOREVER, like you DO, in a Dream.

Then a sound came from thunder, that commanded my stay,

as a Child came from Heaven, to point *out* my new way.

Now his wings were of Glory, and his face

of a Saint.

(I could show you a picture, but I didn't have paint . . .)

I could tell you a story, but I didn't have *words*,

but that Child felt *not* sorry, for He knew I had heard.

He knew I felt SOMETHING, as he drifted away,

For he knew he had heard me, and he knew I could say:

I have witnessed an Angel, that had

sounds of a song,

I have witnessed an
Angel that I *knew*

for so long.

Then the Sky opened wide, to reveal a new land,

That was full of white orchids, and FULL of

white sand.

Now, I sang to the faces of the children of Light,

yes, I sang TO their faces, and I sang to the night.

And the witnesses WITH me, had to hide their disgrace,

as I showed *all my Glory*, and I covered it with lace.

And I asked one fair maiden to uncover her breast,

while I laid there BESIDE her, and put her to test.

ALL THE OILS IN ISRAEL, couldn't replace

the slick,

she created inside her, as she moved

oh, so quick.

And the Maidens around me, gave WOO at the

sight,

as I laid in the solution of Man's Only

Right.

As I lay there so quiet, they would

memoir the days,

when I laid beside THEM, in a thousand

new ways.

(And the seagulls *did* see us, and they dropped us

their due,

as they do when they SEE us, as we lay there all through)

And evening soon darkened, and the

reasons were clear.

The NEW day *was forgotten*,

and the OLD ONE was here.

The NEW was forgot, as a *rash* in *the seat*,

But the Old one was *present*,

as if here to repeat.

(And I moved, oh, so slowly, as to regain my stand,

and remember the White Bird, and REMEMBER the

sand.

Now, the seats were all *taken*, as I wiped clean the

sweat,

and the ladies were *seated* in their DEEPEST regret.

My visions came clear, as I found a NEW SHIRT,

and I covered my Worries, and I covered my *dirt*.

                              Now, this Journey
                    has

                    BROUGHT me quite a
          story to tell,

                              And if YOU try to
                    test it,

                    the   SALT   you   *shall*
          smell.

                              And if you *think*
                    that I'm lying,

                    just to hide an old game,

                              You can go ask
                    my MOTHER, and

                    she'll tell you the *same*.

                              She will send you
                    to a village,

and will say to find
RUTH,

who will guide
you and PLEASE you,

and will *hand* you the
truth.

And she'll *sing*
you a story,

'bout *life's Only Game*,

and she'll say the
SAME THINGS

over and *over* again.

She'll
CONVINCE *you* of one
thing,

(that for certain I SAY),

She'll convince
you of MERCY,

and SHOW you the WAY.

She'll convince you of Heaven, and show you the Light,

and when the World is dying, she'll *show* you it's right.

Yes, when *this* place is melting

she'll show you a sound,

that will *rock* you, and move you,

'til you LIFT off the ground.

And she'll make you feel happy, when you feel

most alone,

And she'll say:

LISTEN CAREFULLY,

to that *God* awful tone.

And she'll say:

"LOOK INWARD,

to see the pure LIGHT,

but *to know* you won't see It,

unless you *feel* right."

"So I TELL you, my friend,

that the journey's a *waste*!

You can listen to MY tale,

and GET the same taste.

You can sit here beside ME,

and hear MY voice wail,

but I surely must WARN you,

it's one scary tale."

Now, the bed that I sleep on,

is relief to my feet.

(As a *drummer* is happy,

when relieved by his beat).

As his tempo does carry *him*,

to places afar,

So *does* my bed drift *ME*,

to places so far.

(While drifting, I'll tell you,

an unusual tale,

of a boat full of lasses,

who had caught the wind's gale).

And they drifted in Mercy,

of God's precious Thought,

and received countless

Blessings,

for the *Love* they had

bought.

They received *countless*

Blessings,

from the love that DID

come,

as the winds tore *inside*

them,

and made their bones

numb.

Now, I PASS you this Fable,

that in Hopes you would SEE,

just *what* this Long Journey,

was DOING to *me*.

To BREAK DOWN my MIND, and to weary my Life,

as I COMPLETE my Journey of Sorrow and Strife.

And the Sky

seemed to play on the Ocean's great stress,

as I seated my Body, and I laid it to Rest.

And I soared on

to Heaven, and Hell *seemed* to GLOAT,

as I realized my fate,

and my Dream,

and my *BOAT*!

(It was all full of lasses that my *paycheck* did hire),

who were willing, and READY, and *never* did tire.

And it seemed they all watched,

as my glory did show,

for they KNEW what they wanted,

and they knew I did know.

As they slithered about me, their flesh in my face,

I wondered what purpose *they had* in this Race.

End Act 5

Act 6

A faint sound awoke me, as the Dawn came anew,

and left me in mem'ry, of the dreams I'd been through.

And a high shrill of laughter

broke out the new Day,

as a lass we called Prudence,

swam on *her* way.

And it left me THREE

reasons to NOT go ashore,

They were Betty

and Bertha, and

Jean, I *adore*.

And we ALL gathered

sadly, as she swam

to the Shore,

for we ALL saw her
LEAVING, to return

here no more.

My Life was not EASY,
as I crawled to my

feet,

but the new sky did
promise

a new day to

meet.

A sudden wave hit us, and it sent us a'whirl,

as a Giant Swan hovered, and DID take a girl.

And I visioned a Thought, as to *find* what to do,

for the Days were no shorter, and I only had TWO.

And an Angel swooped closely, as to give me a clue,

as a Dove of Forgiveness told us *ALL* what to do.

                        And a serpent

of Horror, and an Angel of Light,

retrieved the Great Ocean and *wet* up the night.

                        And a Whale of Desire,

and a Lamb of World Peace, did approach from the

         Heavens, as to make my mind cease.

                        I had called out to

GREET them, but my words all fell near,

                        As an Angel of Mercy

leaned to wipe 'way my tear.

I reeked of an ODOR, of SALT and DEAD FISH,

as I *realized* that *Sorrow*, was to be my *next* dish.

And I *called out* to Heaven,

(in the Lord's Name, I asked),

for forgiveness and Mercy,

as to *complete* my Task.

I wondered if they SAW me, or KNEW me, (as *Son*),

But I only did WAIT, so to SEE if they'd run.

So to WATCH them come help me, if they DID hear

the Call,

But I waited, and *waited*, and they DIDN'T come

at all.

Now, I'VE BEEN called a missionary,

and I'VE BEEN called a Knave,

Now, I'D BE CALLED a *Leader*,

but I ain't all that brave.

And THEY *ALL* laughed *upon* me,

for the One that I *AM*,

as they laughed at the gurus,

or the ones from Siam.

(If they only did KNOW me in the days of my child',

they would KNOW that the Forest *had not* made me Wild).

(They would know all the REASONS for keeping so still,

they would know all the answers, and I'm *sure* that

THEY WILL).

Our Journey does continue,

as the hot sun beats down,

on a boat and three people,

in a *perilous* sound.

And a mystical sparkle,

appeared in the air,

as to show all the people,

that *Judgment* was there.

It created a void,

as to *show* me the *deep*,

and it muttered a *sound*

that was *less* than a peep.

Then it *made* me a Sailor,

and showed me the way,

and I'm *sure* that I
EARNED it,

(after *all* of these days.)

As the boat started
rocking,

all the gear went amiss,

and it scattered about me,

as a lass threw a kiss,

and   I   waited   for something,

to *show* me a sign,

as   the   rain   did   start pouring,

and   the   wind,   it   did *whine*.

And   the   Sounds   of *Forever*, seemed to let out

a *groan*,

as I *fell* to the knees of a *God*-awful tone.

And that tone burned so *LOUD*, that it *burned*

in my *Brain*,

(as the *SALT*, and *the*

SEA, and the *WIND*

and the RAIN).

And it *seemed* to be

saying, in a *Voice*

so discreet,

"If you *Enter* to *Heaven*,

DON'T *FORGET*,

wipe your feet."

And my eyeballs rolled

INWARD,

as my *sight* fell away,

and I witnessed a *miracle*,

ON that *strange* day.

I saw a Bright Ember,

oh, so deep Inside,

that It kissed me, and hugged me, that my Love

could not hide.

Yes, it *kissed* me, and *hugged* me,

as to SEE what I mean,

when I ENTER to Heaven, while *still* in a Dream.

I must TRY to *get* to Heaven, *BEFORE* I grow old,

or I MIGHT miss the *Entrance*, (or so I am told).

I *must* realize the MEANING of God's Perfect Thought,

(as the people respond ALL, to what THEY are taught)

As the people do *GRIP* at the

things that I own,

the Light does burn inward,

the Sound, It does drone.

And I YELLED out to stop all the

                things of my Past,

and I heard,

                "You're Forgiven,

                you can come home

                at Last."

                And I felt ALL the
Blessings of *GOD*

                come Inside,

                as I lay there SO quiet,
that my Love

                could not hide.

                And I lay there, deep
breathing,

                in beat with my
Fate,

as I tried to recall what it

WAS

I had ate.

Now, the noon sun had Calling, 'bout mid-after day,

When It burned all my clothes off, and parched my

'array.'

As it burned dots right THROUGH me, it m*ade* my

mouth say,

In God's Name, *Forgive* me, I have *brought* a new Day.

And a Golden Light
shimmered,

at the *sky's* vibrant light,

and I NO LONGER
worried 'bout

Wrong,

or 'bout Right.

And I had my two ladies and *Dream* to

Fulfill,

as I cancelled my Plans, and I wrote out my Will.

For NOW I REMEMBER God's Most Perfect Plan,

(*"to be in the motion of God's perfect Man!"*)

To create a Purpose, *reflecting* God's Love,

To remember that *Life*, fits with *God*, like a *glove*.

And all your *assumptions* of God's Only Dream,

can't lead *me* to *Heaven*, (if you *know* what I mean) . . .

(And I suddenly REALIZE, here deep in my thought),

that death's not a Dream,

(or so I am TAUGHT.)

SO this MUST be real, and I must be *obsessed*,

(with the idea of *fever*), as I lay here to rest.

THE *REASON* FOR CALLING, IS NO *LONGER* A TEST,

I SHALL *SOON* BE FORGOTTEN, JUST *LIKE* ALL THE REST.

My head clamors Visions, and my Mind *is* a blur,

as Reality STRIKES me, my Body does stir,

And I seem MOST forgetful of the lasses I knew,

as I realize my Fate, and I *know* I am through.

And I try One more time to JUST open my eyes,

but they ONLY look *inward*, to *reveal* my *disguise*.

I have SEEN many Visions, I have seen

MANY Souls,

and I know that I certainly HAVE paid

my tolls.

So I swallow a LAST
TIME, and I *feel*

my heart DIE,

as I CALL OUT to Jesus,
"oh, Lord,"

I ask "WHY."

But He *does not* respond,
as the

Days of *His* Life,

recalled   Him   to
HEAVEN,

where he lives as

THE CHRIST.

Oh I *may* miss the POINT about Religion and things,

but I STILL know a daisy, and I know a bird sings.

I *know* that a LION can sleep in his den,

and I *hope* with *that* knowledge, I can surely get In.

62

And I HOPED with that knowledge, they would SURELY

reply,

but I think that they're WAITING for my *Body* to die.

Again, I see Visions, they won't

leave me alone,

and *again* I hear Sounds, that *resemble*

that *Tone*.

I know not my Journey, (as you'll see what I MEAN),

I am ready for NOTHING, and, I, can't, stop, this, Dream.

And my boat again RAGES,

so FAR in the seas,

as the ladies I'm *carting*,

got *down* on their knees.

And they *begged for forgiveness*,

as if *THEY* had done wrong,

so I Blessed them,

and *kissed* them,

and I *sent* them *along*.

Yes, I blessed them, and kissed them,

and I sent them away,

as I sat there *alone*,

to face MY Judgment Day.

And the boat started ROCKING, and the sky poured out BLOOD,

as I heard thunderous *footsteps*,

my Life *seemed* a dud.

And a smile from the Father,

seemed to BEAM DOWN and say,

"YOU MAY COME *HOME*, MY CHILD,

YOU MAY *COME HOME* TO *STAY*.

And I sighed, oh so softly, at the *sign* of reprieve,

that my Body bucked over, and my Soul took it's leave.

And I seemed to be DRIFTING in a void of my OWN,

where I felt FREE and HAPPY, (but I did feel ALONE).

And as I MEMOIR, (the things in my Past),

I *realized* my worries were LIFTED at LAST.

And a Hand *seemed* to TOUCH me, ('though a hand can't

touch Soul),

when a Voice slowly WHISPERED, that I HAD reached

my Goal.

I understand Heaven, and I understand Hell,

And I *know* why your FAMILY will come *wish you well*.

For they KNOW you are *going* to places so free,

and they *don't* have to PAY you, or *GIVE YOU A FEE*.

No, they *DON'T have to pay you, or CON you to go,*

for the Entrance is EASY, and that we *all know*.

The   Entrance   is

worthless,

(for *MONEY* to buy),

which is *why* you have NOTHING, on the Day that you Die.

Which is WHY all the people gather 'round at your Wake,

to Bless you, and KEEP you, a friend NOW to make,

But they'll ALL make *their* Journey,

as their Story SHALL tell,

but *WILL* it be Heaven,

or *WILL* it be Hell.

Will it be a place where

their Worries shall cease,

or a Kingdom of Horror,

where there SHALL BE
no Peace.

As I open my Story, so it 'be IN my FACE',

all the *World* comes together,

to SEE my Disgrace.

I was LEFT in a coffin, the Wake to ENHANCE,

but the Mortician had forgotten to zip up my pants.

End Act 6

SEQUENCE

As the Story now closes, I bid you adieu,

and I hope I have brought you MORE closer to *you*.

I have joined now, in union, with the Spiritual Sky,

and await YOU, for ALWAYS, 'til YOUR Body dies.

And I hope that in mourning, you will SEE what

    I MEAN,

when I SHOW Life as Roses, as I show you *your* Dream.

We are *all* built of Heaven, as your Body is from Earth,

and I 'wait you, and WANT you, from the Day of your Birth.

And as YOU await Heaven, (or Hell, as they say),

I will SEND you an Angel, as to Lighten your Way.

I will send you a *Guardian*, who will host you along,

as I DRIFT WITH YOU ALWAYS, and I *help* you feel strong.

I DO think that Heaven IS the place you

Should BE,

So *think* of that ALWAYS and

Set your Mind Free.

I will guide you, and PLEASE you,

'til the Day that you DIE,

For I'm *spiritually* HERE,

To *avenge* a Child's Cry.

And I'll call YOU a Child of

YOUR Father of Light,

If you promise to *do* what the Soul

Says is RIGHT.

And I'll help you to live
WELL,

Until your Last Breath.

Then I WILL gather *TO*
you,

At the *time* of your
Death.

EPILOGUE

The mists of *Clear Vision*, now paint in

my VIEW,

as I MEMOIR the things I have SAID HERE to you.

Now ALL is forgotten, of Man's HOLY GAME

for *Man*, and *his* God, are *ALL BUT* the Same.

And riches, and *worship*, all leave *you*

with *NONE*,

but *Union* to *God*, can *MAKE YOU* His Son.

Plus, *Union* in *Spirit*, in Life, in *YOUR* land,

will *GET* you to Heaven, if you reach *out* your Hand.

If you CRY to the Father

to come home to YOU,

I   assure   you,   that
SOMEDAY, your crying

IS through.

And NO MATTER *how*
weak, or how TROUBLED

you BE,

When I GET you to
HEAVEN,

YOU'LL finally see.

When I GUIDE you 'cross *Waters* that *DON'T* run through

your SINK,

you *will SEE it's from Heaven,*

(*if that's what you Think*).

The End

"A PART OF ME"

The Autobiography of
Nathan Charles Sollish

Author of "Evolution is Creation"
and
"All is in a Dream"

For many years, I've wanted to try and express what has happened to me during the course of my life, so here goes.

I was born in Los Angeles, California, on October 5th, 1949, at 12:48PM. My father was born in New York. His father, for whom I am named after, hailed from Bulgaria, and his mother was from what was called in the "old days", White Russia, whatever that means. My mother was born in Texas, as was her father and mother. My Great grandparents on my mother's side came from Germany. To this day, the majority of my mother's side still resides in Texas. My dad was, and remained all his life, a long haul truck driver. When I was born, he was driving for Garrett Freight; soon after, he started hauling the ice making equipment for the world renowned Ice Capades. Not only would he drive all over North America, the company would also ship his truck, and him, to Europe and Asia, where he would follow their troupe to whatever country they were scheduled to perform in. He even was given a very respectable uniform to wear when he drove, to properly represent the Ice Capades. I even recall that he had a very unique tie clip and military style dress hat; very respectable, indeed. When he came home, and brought his truck with him, the Disney characters all over the trailer would draw people like they were coming to look at the neighborhood Christmas lights.

Throughout my childhood, wherever we were, whenever the Ice Capades came to town, we always got in for free, and got the best seats in the house. My dad always had a little reunion with everyone after each show. One time, the cast of the show came off the ice, and grabbed my dad from his seat, and pulled him out onto the rink, and jokingly started sliding him all over the ice. The audience thought it was part of the show. Another time, my dad spent so much time after the show in one of the female stars dressing room that my step-mother got jealous. That particular incident was pretty funny. Going to Ice Capades shows went on for years, even after my father went on to work for other trucking outfits.

Anyway, in those days, long haul trucks didn't have big sleeping compartments like they do these days; they just had a canvas strap that snapped to the back of the seats to form a cot. Underneath it was a cold, barren space that the driver would toss his luggage down into. Sometimes, my Dad would take me for a ride, and I'd lie on the canvas strap, picking at the snaps until I'd pop enough snaps to cause me to fall down into the storage space, below. My Dad would always say, "Where the hell did you go!"Then he'd reach down, and lift me up by my arm, reminding me to not play with the snaps. Secretly, it was my little game that I'd play.

My mother, on the other hand, took advantage of my father's days on the road, by passing herself around to other men, for money. I recall more of my life spent at neighbors homes then at my own. The people who babysat my brothers and myself would drop us back into our house through the bathroom window in the middle of the night, because they were tired of always having us at their house. In most cases, I'd find my mother in bed with a strange man, and a stack of money on the night stand. Sometimes, my mother would leave me with just my older brother, who was just about two years older than me, and didn't understand how to change diapers, or make meals, so we'd be starving, and covered in feces when she got home. She had very little concern, but my father never knew. My older brother, and my two younger brothers hardly knew each other, since we each went to different sitters.

One day, my father was away, as usual, and my mother was out partying it up, also as usual, and my older brother and I were left alone in the house. My younger brothers were at babysitters homes. The next thing I recall, a group of thieves broke in, and stole literally every single thing in the house, and they even washed and mopped the place to cover their prints. They had to know where my parents were, to be able to know they had the time to do this. I also recall them setting my older brother and I in the middle of a barren living room, and telling us that our parents should be grateful that they were not kidnappers. Then they left. After a day, we were starving, and started crawling around, driven by instinct, looking for food. I was about five years old, and my brother, seven. We found a rock hard piece of bread and bottle of hot sauce behind the counter. We then discovered a tube of toothpaste in the bathroom, so we smeared the toothpaste and hot sauce on the bread, and took turns biting off pieces, and eating it. In the middle of this feast, my father pulled up in his Ice Capades truck. When he opened the door, and found us eating the crusty bread in the middle of an empty house, with my mother gone, he blew a fit. Leaving his truck engine running, he put us into his Studebaker, and we immediately began a three thousand mile journey to his mother's house in Brooklyn, New York. Later in life, he explained it was because he needed us to have a secure place with family, while he continued to work to support us.

So, the next morning after arriving, I went downstairs from my grandmother's house, and for the first time in my life, saw concrete for as far as the eye could see. As I stood there in awe, a Puerto Rican boy about my age came up to me, and told me that I was standing on his turf. 1 never heard this expression before, so for some strange reason, I broke out laughing. The kid got all flustered, said, "O.K., it's your turf too", and took off running. I told my dad about it, and he said, "Welcome to Brooklyn". A few days later, a neighbor in California called my Grandmother with the message for my father that his truck, which had been running the entire time, had finally run out of gas. My Dad took me to the neighborhood school, and the teacher introduced me as Nathan, from California. I was immediately alienated. Why did she have to add the "from California" part? Anyway, that neck of the woods was called Brownsville. In the course of time, we moved to the neighborhoods of New Lots, and East New Lots, where I was the only white kid in an all black school. The principle requested that my family relocate me to another school, so they did. Then we moved to

East New York, a neighborhood still in Brooklyn, and then to the Flatbush area, where I went on to finish elementary, junior high school, and high school at Erasmus Hall, also known as just Erasmus, which was located on the locally famous, Flatbush Avenue.

The school was so old that it actually had secret passages in the walls to hide children in, in case soldiers stormed the place. An English class I had, had one. If you went into the book storage closet, and turned a simple latch on the wall, a secret door would open, leading you into a hollow wall, large enough to hide a class of kids. And on the opposite wall was a similar latch. If you turned it, the wall there had a secret door too. This would lead into a broom closet out in the hall, making an escape route, as well. I loved to play tricks on the teacher, because he didn't know about the secret passage. I'd tell him a page was missing from my book, and ask if I could get another one. Then I'd go into the book closet, but return from the hallway. He'd say, "I thought you went into the book closet!" To which I'd reply, "No," I said "the bathroom." He actually never caught on, no matter how many times I pulled the prank.

Now, there's one thing that I forgot to point out about my family. A couple of months after arriving in Brooklyn, thinking my brother and I needed a mother, my dad went out and snagged the first woman he could find, wooed her, and married her. She turned out to be the step-mother from hell. Of course, my Dad could never know that in advance. She hated the fact that my brother and I was from another woman. She'd put crushed glass in our school lunches, make us eat standing up at the kitchen counter, and only allow us the privilege of watching one T.V. commercial a week. No programs. She'd always tell my Dad we had homework, or were bad, and being punished. He never knew that she was setting us up. She'd tell us on the side that if we told him, she'd make life a lot worse for us. When she had a child with my Dad, she treated her child like a king. He got to eat at the table, watch T.V., get new clothes all the time, and go out to eat at restaurants. She'd take us along, but her and her son would eat, while we sat there and watched. All the different store owners saw this, and began slipping us food, and even money to buy food, literally almost every day. My stepmother's reputation grew behind her back, and she never caught on. She'd tell us that she ate in restaurants in front of us so we would know how to do these things when we grew up.

Did I forget to mention that in the course of us travelling to New York, my mother put my two younger brothers in an orphanage? When my dad learned what my mother had done, he contacted the orphanage to retrieve them, but they already adopted off my youngest brother, Michael, and couldn't get him back, and I never saw him again. Michael Sollish, if you're reading this, contact me. My other brother, Bob, was escorted across country by train, by a woman who worked at the orphanage, and delivered back into the hands of his family. My older brother, Tom and I welcomed him with open arms, but the orphanage had already made him robotic. Nothing was ever the same between us.

Now, back to my step-mother. She took my dad's money, and treated herself like a queen, giving us kids the barest minimum to eat, and wear, somehow eluding my dad, the whole time.

By the time I was twelve and a half, I was so hungry, that I went looking for a job. I located a grocery store called "Weinstein's Food Store", and they hired me as a stock clerk, and grocery delivery person. I unloaded trucks, stocked shelves, and pedaled a three wheeled bike that had a giant steel box in front around to apartment houses, delivering boxes of groceries to customers, sometimes huffing them up as many as six flights of stairs. Sometimes I'd get a dime or quarter tip, and sometimes I'd get nothing. The minimum wage was seventy-five cents an hour, back then, but between that and the tips, I made enough to eat. However, I woke up one night, and found my step-mother robbing my tips from my pants, so I figured out how to open the elevator shaft door, and get on top of the elevator. From there, I located areas in the shaft that were missing bricks, and stashed my money in the holes. My older brother got a job delivering newspapers to the teacher's desks at Erasmus. Ironically, the Board of Education learned that I was working instead of attending classes, and never sent truant slips home. So, as it turns out, I've paid into Social Security since I was twelve. Sadly, once I reached sixteen years old, the Board of Education decided that since I spent most of my time at work, they no longer wanted to carry me on the rolls, and asked me to bring my father in to sign me out of school. So, at sixteen, I became a hard working high school drop-out. I decided to change my line of work, so I got a job at Orbach's, a clothing store, in Manhattan. Other than for a girlfriend, my life was pretty isolated.

Once in a blue moon, my dad would take me to see a Dean Martin, and Jerry Lewis comedy, or maybe a western. One time, he took me to Madison Square Garden in Manhattan, to see the Roy Rogers Rodeo. Unfortunately, I sat there and watched a man get stomped to death by a Brahma bull.

Anyway, when I reached seventeen years old, with my parent's un-witnessed signature, I enlisted in the U.S. Army, on October 17th, 1966. Now I was the property of the U.S. government, and my step-mother could no longer affect my life. It was also the first time I had three healthy meals a day in my life. I grew a head taller in two months. After basic training, I was sent to Germany, where I was assigned to The 626th Repair Parts Company. The base was called Pioneer Kaserne, in the little town of Hanau, the very town that the Grimm Brothers, who wrote Grimm's Fairy tales, was from. We repaired everything from submarine periscopes, to a Generals unsprung spring from his ball point pen. Things were pretty boring until they chose me, and six other guys from all over Germany to participate in war games in the Black Forest, in the middle of a very frozen winter. I was part of a squad of six guys who had to continually attack an entire battalion of combat engineers, for an entire month. The loser would have to remain in the field an entire extra month, as punishment. Little did I know that the military had a reason for their madness. I was sent on solo missions every day of the war games, which is the exact type of position I would be given in Vietnam, as I would find, shortly thereafter. We wound up winning the games. Six guys, plus a Buck Sergeant in charge, beat two thousand men. Boy, were they mad!! The war games judges had to sneak us out of there the night before they announced the winner, for fear that the losers would want to tie us to a tree, and pour ice water all over us, and leave us there. It was kind of an unspoken tradition.

About nine months, and a ton of bratwurst and beer later, the Army came looking for volunteers to go to Vietnam. They claimed that there was an enemy build-up occurring all over the country, and they were expecting major attacks any time soon. They soon found out that that was the enemy preparing for the 1968 Tet Offensive, when the North Vietnamese attacked all major cities, and every military installation, all over the country, at the same time. Well, according to military intelligence, the plan that the North Vietminh had concocted was, if they won their Tet Offensive, their next plan was to attack the West Coast of the United States, with full support from the Communist Bloc. Fortunately, they lost that battle. Well, the way it worked out for me, was I had just finished serving one of my three years enlistment, when I found out that there was a re-enlistment program called "taking a short". What that meant was, you'd re-enlist for three years, then they'd drop the remaining two years from the first enlistment, and you'd wind up going from three, to a four year enlistment, with a benefit. But instead of a financial bonus, like one gets for re-enlisting once a full enlistment has been served, a "short" earns the enlistee a choice of immediate re-assignment. So, I re-enlisted for immediate re-assignment to the Vietnam war zone, along with my entire squad. We even made the local German paper. The article read, "Entire squad re-enlists for Vietnam", which included our picture.

Anyway, after a thirty day leave, I was on my way to combat. However, on the way there, I began to have my doubts as to whether or not it was such a good idea. When we landed at Honolulu Airport to change planes, I actually ducked behind some bushes, and watched as everyone loaded onto the plane. I figured I could get lost in the airport crowd, and then merge into society, never to be seen, again. But then, my patriotism got the best of me, and I knew I could never live with myself if I did that, so I jumped out of my hiding space, and joined the remaining people getting on the plane, and finished my journey to what I can only describe as hell on Earth.

On the last leg of the flight, before descending into the war zone, they served us our last civilian meal; Filet Mignon. Being that I came from a poor family, I never had that before, and actually took the offer from a different point of view. I saw it like they were serving me my last meal, period; the dead man's dinner. So I refused it, and went in on an empty stomach.

Well, on January 9th, 1968, as we were landing at Tan Son Nhut airbase in Saigon, now known as Ho Chi Minh City, I glanced out of the aircraft window at hundreds of bomb craters, and wondered what the moon was doing in Vietnam. As we unloaded from the plane, simultaneously, they began loading coffins of those killed, on the same plane, right in front of us. Not a good omen for an eighteen year old boy, straight from the streets of Brooklyn. There I was...old enough to kill, but not to vote or buy beer. Then, they shuttled me to Long Binh, where I found out how the military really works. They took their promise to me, and threw it out the window. They told me that my orders were being changed at the last minute, and I was to hang out until the new ones arrived. Four days later, they did. They changed my job, and my location.

Apparently, I missed the small print that said, if the Army can't fulfill their promise to me, then I agree to take any assignment they need me for. I originally was trained to be a supply clerk. I was also assigned originally, to be at Long Binh, the largest, and most secure military base in South Vietnam. I was reassigned as an armorer specialist, and ammo run for an attack helicopter company in the Iron Triangle; the hamlet town of Phu Loi, in the Phu Coung region. Changing jobs in a combat zone, to one that has to be trained on the job, is a cause for PTSD, because the trauma of entering into a combat role not originally trained for is quite shocking to the system, both physically and mentally. Then, I got a real shocker. They told me, that without a gun, I had to hitch-hike to my new assignment, nearly forty miles away, through winding jungle roads, and when I got there, then they'd issue me a weapon. So, to start my tour, I had to hide in the trees until I spotted an American vehicle, and hope that they didn't shoot me, thinking that I was an enemy soldier jumping out to ambush them. To put it mildly, I was scared out of my wits. I was positive that I was on the road to being shot by my own country. After a long nerve racking day, I got to my company, which was already being engaged by the enemy.

As rockets and mortars fell all around me, I reported in, and begged for a rifle. My unit was Company A, First Aviation Battalion, of the First Infantry Division; a full combat outfit. No one got the day off. The unit's call sign was Bulldogs. Within it were four chopper platoons, Bulldogs, Champagne Flight, Commancheros, and the infamous Rebel Platoon, which sported confederate flags on their shirt pockets, and the doors of their helicopters. My orders showed that I was assigned as a Rebel. I'd like to note that as of 1969, confederate flags were no longer allowed on military equipment. The year that I was there, was the last year that it was allowed. The gunships were loaded with rockets, M-60 machine guns, and mini-guns. A couple of them had automatic fire M-79 grenade launchers attached to the front of the aircraft. The gunships with everything mentioned, all on one ship, was called a "fully dressed hog". When I was doing nothing else,

I had to fly door-gunner. So, I went from working on an assembly line, tearing tags in half in Germany, to a role as an active participant in a combat situation. Not the job, I might add, that I signed up for.

One time, one of the types of missions that I had to fly, when not getting, arming, or issuing ammo, was where the chopper would be located in the middle of, and under four B-52 bombers, carpet bombing a region, so I could observe the under belly of the bombers to make sure the bombs weren't hanging up in the bomb bay doors. As the bombs passed by the chopper, I could read things that G.I.s had written on them as a message to the V.C., like Bye Bye, etc. The concussion from the explosions below rattled the chopper so violently that it was a miracle that the thing didn't break apart. I also had to fly into hot LZ (Landing Zone) areas, get out of the chopper mid-battle, capture VC, and bring them back to the chopper and secure them to be returned for questioning. Those battles were so intense, they were called, "locked elbow to elbow" battles, because there were so many people engaged in battle in such a tight, congested area, that a gun couldn't be used, or the bullet would pass through the enemy, and hit one of our own men on the other side of the VC being shot. Everything was done with knives, and bayonets. You'd have to loop an arm through a V.C.s arm like you were square dancing, pull him to the ground while utilizing your weapon, then immediately do another one, over and over, until the battle was over. I also had to fly what was called "fire support", which meant that we'd cover the ground forces in battle, with fire from the sky.

Speaking of which, at night, we would fly Blackout, which meant no lights, and when the guns were fired, all you'd see was the red tracer bullets coming from the sky, Kind of like lasers; kind of like War of the Worlds. Sometimes, Rebel gunners would fire their machine-guns across the sky to each other's targets, crossing the bursts in the middle, forming X,s in the night sky.

But my main job was being in charge of my company's ammunition, arming it, issuing it, plus ordering it, and retrieving it from the main ammo supply point, which turned out to ironically be Long Binh. A seventy mile solo round trip run, through V.C infested jungle, loaded with booby-traps, land mines, and Viet Cong waiting to ambush the truck they knew held the very thing that would cause their demise...ammo. Upon return to base camp with the ammo, I also had to unload ever piece by hand, by myself .The ammo run turned out to be along Route Thirteen, a dirt two-lane road, also known as Thunder Road, because of how heavily mined the road was, and the even less desired Highway One. On my truck was 2.75 inch rockets, C-4 plastic explosives, claymore landmines, fragmentation and incendiary grenades, bullets, flares, and anything else needed to protect the troops, the attack helicopter company I was in, and the base camp. I was a rolling time bomb, waiting to happen. The total run was about a seventy mile round trip experience beyond comprehension, each and every time. My life expectancy was fifteen minutes.

My ammo run was a solo assignment, so any confrontations that I had with the enemy, I dealt with alone, unless I drove into a battle that was already engaged. Then I had to jump out of my truck and join in, until I could drive through it. The first ammo run I took was the eye opener for me, for the rest of my tour. No one warned me about anything, so I had to learn it as I went. So as I approached a railroad crossing, a group of young teenagers flagged me down, signaling that a train was coming. As I came to a stop, the next thing that I knew, I was gagging, as four of them were suddenly in the cab of my truck, strangling me, and attempting to take my gun, and pick my pockets. It didn't take but a few seconds for instinct to kick in, and I started belting them with every ounce of my strength. Somehow, I got them off of me, and out of the truck. Then, just as quickly, they jumped behind a bush, and popped right back out holding AK-47s.As they pointed them at me, I realized that they were Viet Cong, and grabbed my rifle, firing it in their direction as I floored the gas. I never looked back .That was my welcome to Vietnam. When I got back to the base camp with my ammo, I told the First Sergeant what had happened, and he told me that seven VC or less WAS Vietnam, and to get used to it.

Then he went on to tell me that he was from Alabama, and he'd never let the world think a man from Brooklyn was any kind of war hero, and told me that even if I won the war by myself, he'd never let it be known, and all I'll leave the war with is the two standard medals given to everyone. He fulfilled his threat. For all I did do, as an American in a war, I got no recognition, whatsoever. What a bastard. Anyway, my job was non-stop; first one thing, then the next; over and over, again.

Here's a bit of irony for you...my orders to that unit were issued on January 13,Special Orders #13 , to drive Route 13.I'm not sure if the number 13 was lucky or not, but I am alive, and did make it home without being shot. The ammo man before me, whose place I took, wasn't so lucky. The Viet Cong shot out his truck engine, and when he tried to run for cover, they gunned him down, and killed him. The VC cleaned the truck of all the ammo, and left it there. The Army salvaged it, put a new engine in it, and gave it to me. When I walked over to the truck for the first time, I saw a bullet hole in the hood, but upon investigation, didn't find a scratch on the engine. That's when the motor pool sergeant told me the story.

I eventually had my girlfriend's name, Ellen, painted on the front of the hood, as sort of a good luck feature. I'd like to think that it worked. Because of my multiple job positions, I was usually wearing a tiger-striped camo shirt, door gunner flight pants, a bush hat, and steel toed combat boots, in case ammo dropped on my foot. In my truck, I kept my M-16, and a 40mm grenade launcher, with at least fifty rounds of 40mm ammo. I also wore a 45 cal. pistol for close quarters combat inside the cab of my truck, which happened more often the I would have liked, since the VC would jump from trees onto the truck, and then climb inside. I tried reporting the ambushes to my commanding officer, but it was useless. As time progressed, he would tell me that he sent gunships to the main ambush points, and had them spray the area with gunfire, and implied that they "cleared the area". They either didn't have any idea that the enemy was climbing down into tunnels after each assault, or they didn't care. Finally, I realized that I'm the one with the ability to do something about it. I was the ammo man. I ordered the ammo. So, using the limited knowledge that God gave me, I realized that armor piercing bullets would penetrate deeper into the ground, and have a better chance of travelling deep enough into the ground to hit the enemy in the parts of the tunnels that were close to the surface, so I started ordering it for the door gunners, and for the mini-guns, which were electronically spun Gatling guns that fired 7000 bullets a minute. After a couple of fire passes over the area with the new ammo, the ambushes lessened quite a bit in those areas.

It didn't take much longer for me and other G.I.s to realize that the Brass wasn't as smart as we hoped them to be, since our lives were in their hands. The order that made it all clear was when the enemy was right outside our perimeter wire, and the order came to not fire unless fired upon. Basically, this meant, let the enemy kill you, then come back to life and return fire. From then on, we were put into the position of making last minute decisions for ourselves. I, personally, was luckier than most, because on the ammo run, and in the ammo dump, I was alone, since no one wanted to be around that many explosives. So, all decisions pertaining to my job were mine to make. I found it humorous that everyone avoided the ammo dump, just because it was located on the chopper flight line, and was constantly under mortar and rocket fire. Between that, and the continual onslaught of gunfire, and bullet holes in my truck and tires, I thought I had a pretty safe job. Not. The world shall never know how the days of a combat ammo man is spent, but I will say this...no matter what deeds I had to do, or what tasks I had to perform, the only heroes in war are the ones who gave their all: their lives, for their country.

There was, however, a time when I came so close to the Devil, that I smelled his breath. I happened to be within ear shot of a conversation between the company First Sergeant, and a mommasan that worked for the Army. She was telling him that the VC had just came into her hamlet, and killed her parents, her husband, and her children; because they had learned that she did our laundry. I was shocked to hear the First Sergeant reply, "we have our own dying, and I can't be bothered". I couldn't believe what I was hearing. This woman was risking her life, and that of her family, to prove her patriotism to the Allied Forces, and they shunned her, in the time of her greatest need. I couldn't handle it. I walked over, and quietly told her I'd take her home, and help lay her family to rest, if she liked, as long as the Viet Cong had left. She said they had, so I went and asked my friend Ray if he'd ride shotgun on an unauthorized mission with me. He agreed, so we headed over to the motor pool area to get my truck. I told the motor pool Sergeant the plan, and he agreed to let me take the truck under one condition. I had to agree that if I was caught, he was going to say that I stole the truck. I agreed. So, we headed out into the jungle; me at the wheel, Ray riding shotgun and mommasan in the middle. We came out of the jungle on the backside of the hamlet of Phu Cuong. As I was pulling to a stop just out of the tree line, we met about a hundred Viet Cong, holding their rifles by the tip of the barrel, with the butt swinging just above the ground. As we spotted them, they spotted us. All rifles lifted up, and pointed directly at us. We immediately placed our hands on the window where they could see them. As we watched, VC started grabbing other VC by the arm, and stopping them from firing their rifles at us. Then they started breaking off into the jungle, to our amazement; As the last of them started to disappear into the trees, the last one, the rear point man, turned, and pointed his rifle directly between my eyes, then lifted the barrel upward, turned, and darted off into the trees. I don't know what I was fearing more, dying, or being tortured to death. I knew we were too far from Hanoi to be taken prisoner, and hauled all the way to North Vietnam, to live out the war in the infamous Hanoi Hilton prison for prisoners of war. I looked at mommasan, and said, "You told me they already had left." She said nothing. Apparently, she wanted to exact a little revenge, even though I was the one trying to help her. I asked her to get out of the truck, saying I didn't know if the VC would change their minds, and come back. We determined that the enemy didn't know if there were more trucks, or men behind us, and they didn't want to give away their position by making noise with gunfire.

When we got back to base camp, we had the convenience of being an attack helicopter company, so we went to a couple of pilots we knew, and gave them the VC's position. They made up a mission for the books, went looking, and found the enemy unit, wiping them completely out .So, I guess, if not for the sequence of events that had occurred, we would have never caught up with, and eliminated that enemy force, and many more American soldiers would have died at their hands. Fate has a strange way of getting things done. The following day, mommasan showed up for work, as usual, never saying a word about the incident. We didn't either.

A few days later, I was "volunteered" as part of a team who had to secure an area to be used as a landing area for a paratrooper unit called, "Pathfinders". It turned out to be a graveyard; literally. As we waited for the drop, I watched two water buffalos butt heads, until the larger of the two decided he didn't want me looking, and charged right at me. As its huge horn barely missed my face, I stepped back, and fell right down into a pre-dug grave. The bull looked down at me snorting, as I wondered if it was going to leap down, and land on me. I thought, "GREAT! I'm not dying by the hand of a VC; I'm being squashed by a water buffalo!" Lucky for me it felt content that I was out of the picture, and went back to battle the other beast. A buddy hoisted me out, and didn't let me forget it for weeks. But if you ever want to imagine a somewhat heroic act that I may have done, imagine me standing on the running board of a fully loaded ammo truck, rolling forty miles an hour down a dirt jungle road, while engaged in a fire fight with the enemy, while driving with my foot. True story. Just another day in my personal Vietnam.

However, there were times when things happened, that made the rest a little easier to deal with. Like the time I got blocked from getting back to my base for a night, because of heavy conflicts on the road I had to drive, so I had to spend the night at Long Binh. As I had mentioned earlier, Long Binh was a very large, fortified base camp. It even had flushing toilets, and air conditioning. I was so blissed out by the whole thing, that I wandered into a bathroom, turned all the sinks on, since I hadn't seen running sink water in months, and then, for a goof, lifted the back off of a toilet tank, and started scooping handfuls of water out of it, and drinking it, since it was cleaner water then I'd had in quite a while. As I was doing so, a Captain walked in, and spotted me. It turned out that I had gone into an officer's bathroom without realizing it. He looked at me, all wide eyed, looked at my enlisted rank, looked back at me, and gasped. I think the blood and mud all over me threw him for a loop, if you will. I held up a handful of water, and offered it to him. He said, "no thank you, but please help yourself, then took off down the hall. I'm sure if he's still alive today, so is that memory. That night, I had to break into an enlisted mans club, and sleep on the floor, since no one would let me park my loaded ammo truck near their barracks. Fortunately, while I was there, I discovered a cooler with beer in it, so I admit having a couple before I discovered an electric guitar, and amplifier, to which I again, helped myself. I played until I passed out. The next thing I knew, I was being woke up by two MPs who spotted my truck out back. I thought that they were arresting me, in my blurry state, but then I realized that they were telling me that I could keep the guitar, if I wanted. To my shock, they went on to say that they could tell that I was from "the bush", and compared to me, they had it made, and wanted me to have something. Still half groggy, I explained that we only had electricity from a generator, which we needed to use wisely, since the bigger the load we put on the system, the more gas it took to keep it running, and gas had to be hauled out to our location, which was dab smack in the middle of VC country.

Now, here's where it gets interesting. I decided to take a different exit from the base, and approach the road from a different angle, because of all the gunfire. As I pulled up to the wire along the perimeter, I heard a voice yell, "Chuck?" I looked, and discovered it to be coming from a guy I grew up with in Flatbush, Brooklyn. John "Jackie" Harris. What a rush. For the remainder of my time in Vietnam, I made it a point to stop by and see him, every ammo run. However, like everyone else, his company commander didn't want my truck near him, so we'd meet in an area that stored parts to make bridges, since he turned out to be in a combat engineer company.

Jackie was the only living proof of the hell I personally went through. When he got home, he went on to become in charge of advertising, for Nabisco Corporation. I think that's cool.

When it came time for me to be able to take my three day in-country R&R to Vung Tau, also known as China Beach, the V.C. attacked the place, and I never got to go. But allow me to take a moment to straighten out the meaning of "R&R". Most people think it means, rest and relaxation. Actually, rest and relaxation are the same thing. For those of us in a full combat unit, R&R means Rest and Recuperation. You see, the reason we were given a break, was to recuperate from all the stress laid on us by war.

Anyway, a couple of months later, they let me take my seven day out of country R&R, so I chose Taipei, Taiwan. When I landed, I randomly chose a hotel, and when I got there, the guy at the door taking the baggage turned out to be my older brother, Tom, who recently died April, 2011. He didn't know I was in Vietnam, and I didn't know he was stationed in Taiwan. Weird. So, he wound up taking me to all the neat places, and I got to see my brother, at the same time. One of the more unusual places that he took me was to the top of the Wu Li Mountain, where we enjoyed a day on Green Lake. That is, except for the few tense moments when no one told me the Taiwanese Army had war games there. As we sat peacefully in a rowboat, machinegun fire opened up along the bank of the lake. Being that I was fresh from a combat zone, I dove into the water, yelling for the others with me to join me, as I began attempting to flip the boat upside down, so we could take cover underneath it. They all started to giggle, and revealed to me what was really going on. Very funny. Very funny, indeed. But there was an even more interesting thing about that day. To get to the top of the mountain, we boarded a double bench little rail car on tracks, and was literally pushed all the way to the top by a skinny little old man. The more exciting part of the ride was when we headed back down. After we boarded, he pushed us into the downhill stretch, and jumped on. The car started going faster, and faster, and I really began to worry, because there were no brakes. As we flew down the mountain, and began nearing the end of the tracks, my brother said, "You're really going to love this part". Then, the old man took a bunch of sticks from his pocket, and began shoving them, one by one, under a wheel, filing them down as fast as he shoved one there. My brother told me he was braking. I couldn't see it, and really started watching for the end of the track. But, strange as it was, by the time we reached the end, we were rolling to a stop. Apparently, the guy had been doing it the better part of his life.

Afterwards, we went shopping, to get me a guitar to take back with me to Vietnam. Ironically, two weeks after I returned to war, I was on an ammo run, and when I got back to my base camp with the ammo, I found that my unit had been hit by rockets, and mortars. Thankfully, no one was seriously injured, but as I stepped down from my truck, my friend walked up holding a piece of the face of my guitar.lt was all that was left after taking nearly a direct hit from a mortar. At least I wasn't playing it at the time. A couple of months after my guitar ate it, and since I was the only member of my company who entered into combat on the ground, because everyone else was either door gunners, or gunship pilots, they considered me the most stressed out in my unit, and I was the only one in my company allowed to go to the 1968 Bob Hope Show in Long Binh, since people chosen to go were those of each unit who suffered the most stress. Strangely, I got back to the states in time to watch the show on T.V., and I even saw myself in the crowd. Quite the weird feeling.

The Tet Offensive lasted the entire year I was there; no matter what the newspapers say.lt was nonstop bombardment, relentlessly. Once it started, it never stopped the entire year that I was there, from January 1968 through January 1969. One bit of irony occurred right after battle on July 4th, 1968, Independence Day. As myself, and a few buddies were taking a breather on top of a bunker, suddenly the entire sky lit up. Apparently, the Navy thought it would be a great idea to launch red, white, and blue flares into the air from their ships, to celebrate the 4th of July. What those numbskulls didn't think of, was that it would light the ground like daylight, and give away everyone's position to the enemy. Needless to say, all hell broke loose for the rest of the night, with a lot of casualties, thanks to that blunder.

About four hours after the rampage began, we had another break in the battle. I picked up a guitar, and wrote my very first song.

The name of it was, "Words". Here's the short lyrics: "Words I never really speak of. But I will speak of it today. One that brought to my attention the truthful meaning of life's way. And that word is Freedom. Now, this word is often spoken to me, but it is nothing that I see. Is war a free and loving way, to start out somebody's day? Vietnam is the place that is causing this disgrace." Not much of a hit tune, but definitely how I was feeling at the moment.

Now, my unit was located so close to B-52 bombings, that about half a minute before the bombs hit the ground, we were told to roll up into a ball on the ground, and tighten every fiber of our being, or the air and ground concussion would tear our inner body apart, which is one of the ways that the enemy met its fate. We bounced around like ping pong balls on a ping pong table. The Brass had no concern for the after effects. We were just statistics. In my unit, you didn't get a Purple Heart medal unless they saw blood. A good example was a night during pouring monsoon rains, I was being relieved from perimeter guard duty, when the truck that I was riding in the back of, hit a deep hole caused by an exploding Chinese rocket. The truck slammed to an immediate stop, throwing me into the wall of the truck bed at 30 miles an hour, totally crunching my lumbar area of my back. When the medic arrived, as I worked my way down from the truck, I couldn't hold myself up, because of the pain, and I collapsed. The medic saw my legs give way, and wrote me an order for 24 hour rest for a hurt leg. Then they gave me Lithium, and sent me on my way. But there were so many horrible injuries all around me, that I couldn't possibly complain, even though any injury caused by the enemy is supposed to earn a Purple Heart Medal, and the rocket WAS fired by the enemy!

But since I mentioned the Chinese rockets, I should point out who the actual enemy was. You see, even though we were fighting the Viet Cong, they were supplied with all their armament by the world's largest Communist Bloc; the Czechs, the Russians, and the Chinese. We even killed Chinese and Russian advisers that were with the VC at the time of certain battles. We killed a Chinese advisor once, who was so huge that we laid five Viet Cong underneath him, and you couldn't see them. We were hit by Russian mortars, Chinese rockets, and small arms assaults courtesy of The Russians and the Czechs. Don't let anyone tell you otherwise. And yes, the butt stock of my M-16 did have Mattel stamped on it. They made the plastic gun stock, and Colt made the hardware. After the war, each company was finding that they were losing investors, because they partnered with the other. Gun people didn't want to do business with someone who made toys, and toy investors didn't want to do business with people who made killing machines. So they both agreed to deny that the whole thing ever happened, even though thousands of us had the guns.

Another interesting thing that not many people know about is that Coca Cola also sponsored the war. The way that I found out was a bit unusual. Myself, and my friend Ray stopped at a hamlet one day to "visit a couple of ladies", when the M.P.s pulled in, and arrested us for being in an unauthorized area. They took us to an old jail, built out in the jungle by the French. As we were being led inside, we noticed an old fashion Coke machine sitting outside, just before you enter the building. First, I asked if it was real, since I hadn't seen, or had a cold drink in months. The reply was "yes". I asked if I could get one, and they let me, "for ten cents". It was the kind of machine that you pulled the bottle out of a small door by hand, once the money was paid. Of course, in Vietnam, we paid with Military Payment Certificates, or MPCs. Even the small change. Everything was paper money. Anyway, after purchasing the drink, we headed inside, when I noticed two unique features. First, I noticed a three inch thick electrical cord, leading from the back of the machine, up into the trees, then heading off into the jungle. I asked how come the cord never got discovered by the VC, and cut, and who picks up the empty bottles. The MP replied, "Don't ask." As we walked on past the machine, I glanced at the back of the machine, and saw a multiple plug outlet, factory installed, attached to the motor, made to tap into, and run an entire building, if you had the machine. And that's what gave the jail its electricity. Politics. Anyway, when we got inside, they called our company on the radio, to let them know where we were. They then put us into a ten foot by ten foot cell, that had at least twenty other G.I.s in it. To make it more miserable, the window and cell door was each half boarded up, and it was a hundred and ten degrees outside. Inside the cell, people were taking turns letting each other sit on the one bench that was in there. After a while, they offered Ray and me a seat. As the two guys who were sitting there stood up so we could take their place, we noticed a very strange omen carved into the wall. First, I should point out that I've always gone by the name "Chuck" all of my life. It's a nickname of my middle name, Charles. Anyway, as we were about to sit down, carved into the wall, right where we were about to sit was the words, "Chuck and Ray were here", in large letters. No one in the room knew our names, so it wasn't possible for anyone to play a joke, and carve it there when we weren't looking. I looked at Ray and said, "I guess we're supposed to be here". It's difficult to describe the look on his face. In the long run, all turned out well. The company sent a truck to pick us up, and nobody ever mentioned it again.

As my time got short, and I was nearing my rotation date, I started to get a bit nervous that I was going to get killed, right when I was about to go home. It was common for people to feel that way, as their time to leave approached. So, to keep myself pre-occupied, I volunteered for short range recon patrols, also known as SRRP. We'd patrol outside the base camp perimeter, and locate enemy sniper nests, and pungi pits, which were deep holes with spikes sticking up in the bottom, that the VC would conceal with branches.It was a horrible way to die, if you fell into one. Not that death, in itself, isn't horrible.

Now, let me put one thing to rest about the reason we were in Vietnam to begin with. A lot of people thought that the Vietnam War was a civil war between the North and the South, like our own Civil

War. Not so. The North Vietminh were attacking the South Vietnamese nation to overthrow it, and force it into Communist rule. The North Vietnamese military was supplied by China, Russia, and Czechoslovakia, the major Communist nations, who gave them all of their armaments. Even though we were physically fighting the North Vietminh, we were actually fighting off the spread of Communism. The North Vietnamese were killing men, women, and children, in hopes of striking such a fear into the South Vietnamese, that they'd surrender their lives, freedom, and country to Communist rule, in order to not be killed. That's why we were there.

America has never been a war monger nation. We do not go to other countries to overthrow them, and make them ours. However, we do go to other countries with a show of military force, in order to stop those countries from coming here, and making us theirs. Never forget that it takes that kind of action to keep America free. Nothing else will work, as long as countries exist that want to take over other countries. You have got to remember that, and believe in your national defense system. The Defense Department can't tell you all of their plans, without revealing them to the enemy, as well. You have to have the faith that the military has had enough experience to know what the enemy plans to do, and what they have to do in order to keep them from coming here, killing everyone, and claiming everything for their own. Many wonderful Americans have died so you and I can comfortably sit there, and read this, to say the least. Never forget that there are people right now, dying in order to keep America a free land. Don't let them down again. Don't treat them like people wrongfully treated the Vietnam Veteran, because it's a wound that truly never heals.

Now, I shall continue with my personal history. Just before I left my unit to board the chopper that was to take me to the airfield that had my ride back to the states waiting, my buddies asked me what I was taking home that was Vietnam, since there was no other place in the world like it. I thought for a moment, then closed my eyes, and squatted to the ground. Then, with my eyes still closed, I brushed my hands along the ground, and grabbed the first thing that each hand touched. I stood and looked in my hands. In each hand was a piece of shrapnel. One was a piece of Russian mortar, and the other was a piece of Chinese rocket, with Chinese characters clearly marked on it. How ironic that I picked up the actual evidence I would need to prove who it actually was that we were fighting.

The day I flew out of Vietnam to go home, I got the ride of my life. Not because I was finally on that freedom bird heading home, but because as the plane accelerated down the runway, mortars began shelling the end of the runway, and to avoid being blown up, the pilot floored the gas, and pointed the nose of the plane straight up, or as straight up as possible. The flames leaving the engines trailed way behind the tail of the aircraft, and the ride had to be as close to taking off in a rocket ship as possible. People inside jokingly were yelling that they'd give anyone ten bucks, if they could walk to the front of the plane, which was physically impossible, due to the G-force, and angle of the vehicle. We were at three thousand feet before we ever left the airport. What a ride!! However, we burned so much fuel during the lift-off that we had to land at Wake Island air base to refuel.

Well, on January 10th, 1969, twenty-three hours after leaving Vietnam, we landed in California. A Colonel met us at the terminal, and offered us a steak to celebrate our return. I'm embarrassed to say that I blurted out, "I saw enough meat for one year", and walked on to catch my plane to New York. Once I landed in New York City, I should have realized things were going to be different when no one was there to greet me. I grabbed a cab, and right off the bat, the new war attacked me. An irate driver behind my cab apparently didn't like cabs, or servicemen, I never found out which, and started ramming into the back of us, as we drove down the highway. We finally eluded him, and I got let off in Brooklyn. I grabbed my duffel bag, and headed on home. I thought.

My step-mother opened the door part way, stated, "Oh, it's you, come back when your father's home and slammed the door in my face. The stories about the war had certainly affected her opinion. When my father did come home, I found that his hair had gone from jet black to snow white. He was the only one who truly worried about me the entire time that I was in Vietnam. The people's response to Vietnam had just begun, and to this day, has never ended. Anyway, I took my bag, and headed out to meet my girlfriend, Ellen, who I had been faithfully writing for a year. As I got to Nostrand Avenue, the street we decided to meet on, my sixth grade teacher, Mrs. Feinstein spotted me, and walked over, and with sincere concern, asked me if I was alright, and welcomed me home. I didn't realize at the time, how much I would appreciate that welcome, or that it would turn out to be the only kind and sincere personal welcome I would ever get, because right after that, an elderly lady approached me and said, "What a lovely tan. Where have you been, Florida?" I replied, "No, ma'am, I just returned from Vietnam". She gasped out, "Oh my God" and literally took off running down the street. Immediately following that number, my girlfriend approached. She was the one whose name I had painted on the front of my ammo truck. It turns out that she didn't have the heart to tell me by mail with a "Dear John" letter, so she waited until I got home to let me know that, to put it mildly, she had found someone else. A drug dealer. My family wouldn't let me in, and my girl had left me. Welcome home.

The outrage of insults have literally gone on for decades, and even though the American people seem to accept the fact that they did a horrible thing to their servicemen, there are still many to this day, who toss insults from time to time, as though it was the soldiers fault that the troops were pulled out of that war, instead of admitting that it was their own wining that they don't want to go, that brought about the withdrawal of troops from Vietnam. And to add insult to injury, they opened the door to allow the Communists to successfully invade, overthrow, and claim a once democratic nation, forcing the population to serve their politics in return for their very lives, land, and all that they ever owned, and worked for all of their lives.

Anyway, the first night back, I slept on the roof of an apartment house, in the winter. Actually, I made it my home away from home while I was on leave, before reporting to my next assignment.

Originally, they assigned me to a base in Colorado, but I had heard that there was an office at the Pentagon that a G.I. could go to, to dispute his orders, so I figured, what the heck, and I went to see for myself. I actually succeeded in getting my orders changed to Fort Dix, New Jersey. At this point of my life, I was a bit disgruntled with war, and wound up hooking up with some peace organizations who had opened an anti-war G.I. coffee house, right off of the base. Ironically, the only place that they could rent, was directly across the street from the New Jersey State Police barracks. We had a little fun with that, though. We put out a weekly newspaper called "Shakedown", and since we had a clear view of the front stairs of the police barracks, we'd photograph troopers walking down the stairs, catching them in awkward positions, and put their picture on the front page, entitled, "cop of the month". At first, it outraged them, but after a few issues, they'd always come over, and ask who the cop of the month was, that issue. A couple of times, they even slipped into the coffeehouse and planted drugs around, but luckily we'd always find and discard them. They even got into the habit of parking their cop car just off of our property, at the end of our driveway, and would wait for one of us to leave. Then they'd automatically pull us over, and write us a bogus ticket, to harass us. We'd always go to court to pay the fines in our military dress uniforms, decked out with our war medals, so the judge would know that we were war veterans, expressing our legal right to free speech, and freedom of the press.It was a never ending harassment that never went away the entire time that we ran the coffeehouse. Anyway, all of us at the Fort Dix Coffee house, as we'd call it, decided to put together a peace rally, and I became the antiwar Vietnam veteran spokesman, who spoke at colleges, concerts, and gatherings, to bring people to the base for the rally, continually stressing that we wanted to keep it totally peaceful. Little did we know just how successful it would be. According to the New York Times, in October of 1969, in Wrightstown, New Jersey, right outside the perimeter of Fort Dix, eight thousand people showed up. Here's the kicker...it turned out to be the only one hundred percent peaceful petition, in history! It also turned out to be the largest group of individual organizations to ever come together for a common cause, in history! And, to top it all off, using 100% peaceful tactics, we walked a quarter mile onto the base, making it the first time in American history that an Army base was ever overrun in the Continental United States! Even though I was in the military at the time, and believe me, the brass knew what was going on all along, they didn't do anything to me, because I never wore my uniform and kept my name out of the limelight when I did my public speaking. I was totally legal. The military spokesman for the bases post information offices only quote was, "It was a hell of a fine march!" It was all printed with photo, on the front page of the New York Times!! The photo showed people, for as far as the eye could see. And no one got a Peace Prize!! Ironic!

Jumping ahead for a minute, twenty years later, I went to the twenty year Tet Offensive reunion in Richmond, Virginia. I met General William Childs "Westy" Westmoreland, and got a picture taken with him. As I was getting my picture taken, a guy with a gun jumped out of nowhere, and tried to shoot the both of us. Fortunately, Westmoreland's security tackled the guy before he could squeeze off a round. I looked at "Westy" and asked, "Doesn't your war ever end?" He replied, "Nope". When I got home, I found a letter waiting for me in the mail from the General. He said, "I hope you enjoyed the reunion as much as I did". That guy had a fearless sense of humor.

Anyway, in September of 1970, after serving four faithful years in the military, I was discharged from the Army with the rank of Specialist fourth class, with two dollars in my pockets, due to lost records. I sat down on a bus stop bench to think about what to do, and wound up falling asleep, only to be awoken by a cop kicking me in the stomach, while screaming how I made the Army look bad. Welcome home. Bewildered, I stuck out my thumb, and hitch-hiked across the country to California and looked up an Army buddy. I had never been homeless and broke before, nor had I ever been kicked by a cop. And I certainly never hitch-hiked across the country before.I was still trying to get over Vietnam, but apparently a part of Vietnam I didn't know existed, had followed me home, and was waiting to attack the minute I thought I was safe.

After a week of sleepless, freezing nights on the road, I found my buddy in California, and he put me up. Before getting totally involved in civilian life again, I decided to look up my natural mother who I hadn't seen in well over a dozen years. I found, and called her, and let her know that I was coming for a visit. The conversation was, to say the least, a bit awkward. I arrived to find that I had two more half brothers, and a half sister. That part was nice, but then reality sunk in. My mother had lost all connection to the children that she had abandoned. On top of that, she had become a "neighborhood mom" who handed out money to all the Mexican kids in the neighborhood. However, she made it clear that I couldn't stay the night, so I left after bonding with my two brothers, and sister. She probably would have never looked for me, if I hadn't called her. A couple of years later, my brother Bob tried to visit our birth mom as well. She put him out onto the street, too. So not knowing where I was located, and with nowhere to go, he joined the Marines. Anyway, while staying with my Army buddy, I did odd jobs to pay the rent, and eventually, I bought a guitar and started expanding my songwriting abilities. I began tossing lyrics to Claridge Productions, in Hollywood. They're the people who discovered Frankie Valli and the Four Seasons.

In 1971, I met my wife, Darlene. We were married on May 13th, of that year. Her step-mother was the sister of the famous musician, Carlos Santana's mother, making him my cousin in law. Sadly, we never met, but I did meet his Mom, my Aunt. My wife and I had a son, Aaron William, born March 26th, 1972, who passed away three months later, on June 5th,1972. They told us that a lot of guys who were in the Tet Offensive were giving birth to children who were dying of what they were calling, "crib- death". They said it had to do with the amount of poisons sprayed on us that we ingested. Thanks for the memories. Soon after, my marriage fell apart. Then Paul McCartney bought the company I was writing for, and that went away, too. I headed back to my apartment, only to watch the entire floor I lived on, explode, with me less than a minute from being at my door. Some guy committed suicide, but they never determined how. It turned out to be the largest unexplained explosion fire in the history of Los Angeles, at the time.

All this was just too much pressure for me, so I threw a blanket over my shoulder, and wandered off into the Big Sur Mountains of northern California. I began a life of transcendental meditation that eventually led me to personally meet the Guru Maharaji from India, and two of his Mahatmas. Mahatma Jagdeo, and Mahatma Guru Charananda. I was in the audience waiting to listen to the Guru, at the University of California in Berkeley, when I was asked to accompany the Guru to and from his chair from which he spoke. This is a great honor, because in that Faith, it is considered being in the presence of an incarnation of God. Then they asked me to drive the car with all seven of his Mahatmas in it, when they all went to the airport, to leave to go back to India. As a matter of fact, as I pulled the car with the Mahatmas in it up to the curb to unload, the car with the Guru Maharaji pulled along side of me, and his window rolled down. He looked across at me with a long steady, spiritually loving gaze, before he went on into the airport terminal to catch his plane. My spiritual meditations only got deeper, and more meaningful, as reflected in my book, *"Evolution is Creation"*.

Soon afterwards, I earned and saved money doing odd jobs, and playing music at cafes and taverns, and bought myself a ticket to Hawaii. Keep in mind that back then, a ticket cost a hundred and ninety- nine dollars, one way. I travelled between Oahu, Maui, and Kauai. The last island actually being Oahu, where, in 1977 I landed a PBS T.V. show I called, " Music Session", where I showcased local talent.

One interesting thing that happened while I was there that I'd like to share, is I was staying on an Oahu beach park in a tent, spending time spear fishing, and sunning, basically enjoying my life, for a change, when I decided to walk to the store for groceries, and so I zigzagged my way through the stores to reach the market. Doing so, I avoided the crowded traffic, flowing in and out of the parking lot. This time, it also caused me to miss seeing a lot more. As I approached the market, a car screeched to a stop right next to me, and the driver's door flew open. Out stepped a man wearing a stocking mask, and brandishing a sawed off shotgun. I gulped. He froze in his tracks, turned and looked at me, and lifted off his mask. I thought, "Great! Now that I've seen his face, he's gonna shoot me, for sure!" Instead, he smiled, and said, "Brother, you just walked into the middle of a filming of an episode of "Hawaii 5-0". My heart sunk back into my chest from my throat, as I smiled back. The actor turned out to be Terry Kiser, who later went on to star in the movie and sequel "Weekend at Bernies" and "Weekend at Bernies 2". He wound up taking me around, and introduced me to the star, Jack Lord, who graciously gave me his autograph. I also got the opportunity to meet Jack Lord's stand-in, the person they show from behind, wearing a wig, and padded clothes to look like Jack Lord, so they don't have to pay him for that scene. In some cases, they'd have him dub in his voice into the scene at a studio, and the stand-in does jaw motion to make it look like talking. The most unique thing about his stand-in is that his stand-in was a petite, blonde woman. In wig, and padded suit, one couldn't tell. But as far as my stumbling onto the set, everyone on the set thought it was quite funny, since that sort of thing just doesn't normally happen. Had I not zigzagged behind the stores to avoid the traffic, I would have taken notice to the half dozen CBS trucks, all the cameras, the snack tent set up for the crew, and the crowd watching the filming, who I might add, thought that my escapade was part of the movie. Terry was playing a character called, "Augie", a gangster.

Well anyway, I stayed in Hawaii from April '76 through April '77, when my brother, Bob, who I finally made contact with, wrote and told me he was getting out of the Marines, so I agreed to meet him at the Grand Canyon, and together, move to Oregon.

I want to note that in 1976, just before going to Hawaii, I hiked to the bottom of the Canyon, and again in 2001.The first time I hiked in, it took me four hours to reach the bottom, and eight hours to hike back out. The second time, it took me eight hours to reach the bottom, and two days to hike back out. Time does take its toll on the ol' bod, that's for sure!!

Anyway, Bob and I worked together for a while, and I even took some courses at the community college for T.V. and stage make-up. I'm not really sure why I chose that field. I guess I figured it might come in handy in the field of show biz, sometime. Then I decided to take a trip to Los Angeles, to see if I could land any music gigs. After scouting around as my own agent, I discovered a private show business club, strictly for those who ran, and made up the industry. It was called the Roof Garden Club. It hosted a stage show called, The Yesterday Show, which was exactly like the Johnny Carson Show, later hosted by Jay Leno. The reason the Carson Show was identical, was because one day, he sat in for the host of the Yesterday Show, and got discovered. He was offered his own show, and as a special thanks to show biz, he modeled his show after the one he was discovered on, right down to the split in the curtain. All of the old black and white films of all the old entertainers doing shows on stage, like Jack Benny, Abbot and Costello, The Three Stooges, and so on, were all filmed on the stage that later held the Yesterday Show set. So anyway, I got talking to the director, who thought that my being an anti-war Vietnam veteran, as well as a musician, might make for a great act, and I got booked on the show. So, on Thanksgiving night, 1981, I made my debut. I opened the show with a song, chatted with the host and other guests then closed the show with a song. After the show, I was told, "Welcome to Show Business", by the entire cast and crew. Then, on December 28th, 1981, with the Yesterday Show as my reference, I headlined solo at the world famous Troubadour, in Hollywood, without any audition. My first ticketed performance.

In Oregon, I had a neighbor named Mickey Newbury, who was a well established songwriter in Nashville, who wrote songs for every famous entertainer in country music. When he got one of my tickets to the Troubadour, he looked at it for a moment, and then giggled. I said, "Mickey, what's so darn funny!" He replied, "You're on the ticket with Sticky Wicket!"And then he giggled some more. I probably should add that I didn't use my family name. I performed under the stage name of Chuck Nathan, as a harmonica/guitar soloist instrumentalist. I derived my stage name by using the name I always went by, "Chuck", a nickname of my middle name Charles, and added my first given name, "Nathan", as the last name of my stage name. Hence, "Chuck Nathan". Eventually, I learned of so many people in the music industry with the given name of "Chuck Nathan", that I decided to combine both names as one word. Hence, "Chucknathan". I spent the next twenty years travelling around the United States, performing at outdoor, and indoor concerts, taverns, clubs, and even parties, and reunions; always as a soloist. I even went out of my way to find pipeline towns that were built just for the time that the pipeline was being laid out, because they didn't have any outside entertainment, and really appreciated it. The tips were great, and I had no trouble at all supporting myself. And I met some really wonderful, hard working folks; the heart of America. Of course, when I wasn't playing music, I got odd jobs that fit the season. For instance, landscaping. I'd also cook in restaurants, do handyman work, and even do janitorial, when nothing else was available.

As I stated in the beginning of this autobiography, I started working at a very young age, so supporting myself was nothing new to me. If I had to stand on a busy street corner, and play my guitar and harmonica to passer-bys for tips, I would do whatever it took to stay afloat.

Then, my life began to take a change. With the help of the Disabled American Veterans, who acted in my behalf for my V.A. claim in 1996, decades after I began filing for my service connected benefits, the Veteran Administration finally notified me that they had determined, after many medical exams, that I suffered from what they were calling "Combat PTSD", or post traumatic stress disorder and declared me service connected. Of course, the V.A. didn't admit it right away, hoping to save themselves a few bucks, so the D.A.V. took my case to Washington, D.C., and presented it on a national level. My case was actually settled in a couple of hours. So anyway, they also clarified the fact that I received the Vietnam Gallantry Cross, and a silver service star on my Vietnam Service Medal. I decided to buy a home along a river in Oregon, and did so.

About a year after I bought it, a man who lived on the other side of the highway from me, started stalking my home, and the police refused to come out and investigate. They implied that I was having a country feud with a neighbor, and told me to work it out, myself. Of course, being born in Los Angeles, and being raised in Brooklyn, I was far from the type of individual that would Hatfield and McCoy someone. I continued to call the police, and they continued to refuse to come out. This went on literally, for months. I was distraught with dismay that no one would listen. Especially the police. Had they come out, and talked to this guy, he would have realized that the police were aware of the fact that he was stalking me, and my home, and probably would have ceased coming across the highway to stalk me, and he probably would still be alive, and I wouldn't have been put into the situation the police allowed to happen. Personally, I would have much rather the assailant be in jail for stalking me, and trespassing onto my property. I tried telling the guy to leave me alone, but to no avail. One day, I saw him hauling wheelbarrow loads of fertilizer across the highway, and dumping it along side my well. He claimed it was his garden. Of course, there's no way that he legally could do that, but because the police weren't coming out, he continued on with his plan. He put a few tomato plants in the ground, and began watering fertilizer into my drinking water. The water in my home started coming out brown from the tap. An important note is that I bought my home on the G.I. Bill, and the Veterans Administration sent a health inspector out to examine the well, to make sure that it passed all health codes. One thing that it had to be, was at least fifty feet from any sump, or fertilized ground. So had a garden been there, the well would never had been approved. The fact of that matter is, the well was placed where it was, because that was the only place it could be, in order to meet those needs. The guy putting the fertilizer there was well aware of that, because he had to abide by that very law, in order to put in his own well, on the other side of the highway, where he lived. Still, the police wouldn't come out. Being that my home was in the country, fifty miles from the city limits, it was too much of a hassle for them to come out. They literally are the reason the incident continued to transpire. Then, one day, the stalker waited outside my home, and when I was leaving to go to the store, he attacked and tried to kill me. Living so far out of the city limits, it was easy for him to merely look left, and right, and see that there was no one around, making his attack unwitnessed. I managed to flee back into my house, where I grabbed an old target rifle I had, and told him to leave. He replied that he was coming to get me, so I fired in his direction.It hit his shoulder, but being a target round, known as a CB22 short, it had little effect, and he charged right at me. I fired a second time. This time, it hit his lower neck, bounced around, and randomly hit a vital artery. In the last moment of his life, he turned and wandered over by my well, where he fell, and died. The State claimed he was shot, while watering "his garden", even though it was an illegally placed garden on my property, and he was trespassing to begin with, and wasn't at the "garden" when the rounds were fired in self-defense, either. They were more concerned that I used force that they reserved only for police, not citizens, even though all Americans have the right to self defense, when their life is in danger, as mine was. I then had to deal with the fact that because the police wouldn't respond, I was put into the position of having to take a life, though unintentional. And having to live with it for always. Plus, what I didn't know, was Oregon doesn't have a self-defense law that protects homeowners who may need to use lethal force to protect their lives, and home, outside their front door, and actually hate the thought that someone would think that they have the right to self-defense with lethal force, even when absolutely necessary. They charged me with his death. I also didn't realize that Oregon had a mandatory minimum "one size fits all" law. They charged me with murder, and gave me the same sentence that they'd give someone who dedicated themselves to killing people, even though I never had a police record all of my life, and never intended the guy any harm, to begin with. He stalked me. I didn't go looking for him. I was legally defending my very life. But the court sentenced me to life, with a minimum of 25 years, which means that I'm eligible for parole in 25 years, but in no way means that they have to grant it. And the twenty five year time span will leave me at 77 years of age. An age the average person in my family never lives to see. Basically, as I see it, they killed me. They made it so I have to remain in a prison, and wait to die. A total mental torture, for saving my own life, because the people hired to protect me refused to do their job. At each level of my appeals, each judge presented a different story of what was supposed to have happened, according to the State, which proved unto itself that they never had any sound evidence against me, to begin with. The trial judge claimed I shot the assailant while he watered his garden. The post conviction appeals judge claimed that the assailant knocked on my door, so I shot him. The Appeals Court judges claimed that the assailant glared at me from across the highway, so I shot him. None of the courts had any concrete evidence on me, what so ever. I was the only one present at the time of the incident, other than the assailant, himself. With absolutely no witnesses, the court had nothing at all, so rather than accept the fact that I did, in fact, defend myself from a stalker, they responded with the story that I couldn't have. Then, at the trial, while choosing jurors, the district attorney made the uncanny statement that no Vietnam veterans could be in the jury, because they would all lie for me, since I was a Vietnam veteran. This instantly tainted the jurors to think that the mere fact that I was a Vietnam veteran made me an automatic liar. So, at that point, everything I said was never believed to begin with. I never had a chance for a fair trial, from the very start. As a matter of fact, the courts own case against me proves they never had a true case to begin with. If I changed my own story that much, it would be proof of a fabrication, but the court can do it and get away with it, even though it proves way beyond a shadow of doubt that they never had a case against me, to begin with. And to add insult to injury, every appeals level judges final ruling was the same: Affirmed without opinion, what that actually means is, they chose to agree with the trial judge's decision without ever reading any evidence that I was submitting in my behalf. In actuality, that type of judgment is illegal, since they ignored all facts, in order to make those decisions. But, in Oregon, apparently they can do that. It is living proof that a house divided cannot stand. As long as each state can have its own opinion of the law, this nation shall continue to falter. For all the good I've done, and all the people I've helped, this is what the State of Oregon has done to me, as I sit here now, writing this in a cell in the Oregon State (OSP) Penitentiary.

It's been eleven years now, as of this day of January 9, 2012, forty-three years to the day, after arriving home from Vietnam, and no one seems to care, or wants to get involved. To add insult to injury, the Army review board decided that my Vietnam Gallantry Cross was unauthorized. So, I began the battle to save my award, and since they were saying that the medal, itself, was unauthorized, all the other guys medal, as well. After many months of through the mail debate, they finally said that since the President of that country did, in fact, give me the medal, and it was backed up by paperwork from the Department of the Army, that the medal was authorized, after all, and it was mine, and I was allowed to wear it. Talk about a long range kick in the butt! Of course, that was after I had sent them copies of the very paperwork that they had originally gave me, to begin with. How very offensive, to say the least. What other insults could the government lay on me, I thought to myself. I was certainly about to find out, in the worst possible way. I never had a police record all my life, and I was never a troublemaker, or a violent person. They don't care that my writings have been in the Library of Congress since the '70s. They don't care that I was honored in Oregon Department of Veteran Affairs historical book, entitled "150 years of Oregon veterans". (However, they accidentally listed me as having been in the Marines, instead of the Army, but all other facts are 100% correct, as written on page 191 in that book). They don't care that I had a T.V. show in Hawaii, or that I performed music all over the United States, or that I personally was the headliner act at the world famous Troubadour in Hollywood, California December 28,1981.0r that I lived a life believing in peace. I remain merely a statistic in the minds of the Oregon law, and to them, I never was, and never will be important, or worth caring about.l am, in their eyes, whatever the judge made me out to be, and that's how they've treated me, ever since.

And so, in closing this autobiography, I want to note that I've earned my GED high school diploma. I've been legally ordained as a Pastor, and I've published a book, entitled, "Evolution is Creation", (available online, and through your local bookstores.) And that I never meant to harm anyone, and certainly don't deserve to die here. At this point of my life, it appears that the soloist musician Chucknathan, my stage name, has disappeared off of the face of the Earth, as has the war veteran, and writer, Nathan Charles Sollish, my given name. God help us all. May God bless us and keep us, everyone. And remember- there's no self-defense law in the State of Oregon that protects a homeowner who may need to use lethal force to save his life, his family's life, or his home. Their law actually says that the assailant has to be attacking you inside your house, which is actually saying that outside your front door, the assailant can point a gun at your head, and you don't have the right to feel life threatened. Basically, it appears that an assailant can go around harming and threatening whoever they want, in any way they want, so long as they don't do it inside your house. America, you have to wake up. This same thing can happen to you. They can't say when a human being can feel threatened. That's a personal feeling that occurs on an individual basis, according to each individual circumstance. And America needs to also realize that Oregon's Measure 11 mandatory minimum law is a one size fits all law that does not take into consideration the circumstances of each individual situation. They gave me, who warded off an assailant who died while threatening my life, the same sentence that they'd give a career killer, when I didn't deserve to be sentenced, at all. I always lived within the boundaries of the law. I know that I'm a good person, and a good American. I've literally spent my lifetime being kind, and helping people whenever I can.

Plus, compared to the creeps I've met in this place, I'm nearly a Saint. But once you're in prison, the way that they treat you is based on the point of view of the judge that sentences you. The court provides an attorney that actually works for the State, and never intends to truly represent the defendant to begin with. The one they appointed to me, made the statement, "somebody died, so somebody has to go to jail, and you're the only one left", before he ever reviewed my case. They just fill the roll, so it can't be said that an attorney wasn't provided. If a private attorney can't be afforded, then there is no chance for a true and honest trial. Once in a prison, the hell never ends. The best thing to do is remain as invisible as possible. I'm beginning to worry a little more, now. I may be sixty-three, but I look well over my age. The stress is continual. The young punks being imprisoned these days, love assaulting old people. And again, no one cares, or wants to get involved. As far as they're concerned, "what happens in this prison stays in this prison." Well, I submitted a petition to the Governor, requesting that he at least commute my sentence to time served, but I don't have high hopes about it. I did the same thing with the last Governor, and all his secretary did was send a standard form letter stating it was denied. He has staff that handles that stuff in his name. I discovered that after receiving the notification letter that my petition was received this time. I got out the one I received from the last Governor, two years ago, and it was exact, word for word. I have to wait six months before I get a verdict, but when I do, I'm sure it will be the short, blunt, word for word statement that I don't qualify. (Update: I received the Governors answer, and as expected, it was a standard denial form letter.) It's obvious that they put the date the Governors answer is due into their computer, and a week before it expires, the computer prints out the letter. And it was exactly, word for word, like the one the last Governor sent. I'm quite sure that they never read a thing. They just do what they have to, in order to appear that they are fulfilling the obligation of the office of Governor.

Well, you've read about the quickest version of my life that I've ever lived. I never tried to sum myself up in a few pages, before, but I hope I gave you, the reader, a glimpse of my world, as it was presented to me by God, or Fate, whoever, or whatever is out to test me, and make my life miserable. Some other more interesting experiences of my life are mentioned in Chapter Three of my book, *"Evolution is Creation"*. As a final note, I just want to say that I've never meant anyone any harm in life. Maybe the good really do die young. I hope not. But for now, for all that I've been through, here I am, all alone, waiting for you. Thanks for reading.

Nathan Charles Sollish, author

Nathan Charles Sollish was born October 5th, 1949, in Los Angeles, California. At the age of five, he moved to Brooklyn, New York, with his father, and two brothers, where he resided until 1966, when he joined the Army. He was Honorably Discharged after serving four years, in which time he did a 9 month tour in Germany, and a year tour in Vietnam, throughout the entire 1968 year of the Tet Offensive war, with the U.S. Army's' 1st Infantry Division.

After the military, he married, and lost a son at a very young age, due to the poison his body absorbed while in Vietnam, that passed to his sons' frail, newborn body. His son, Aaron William Sollish, died at a young 3 months old; shortly their after, his marriage dissolved. From then on, Nathan learned how to play the guitar and harmonica, simultaneously. As an instrumentalist, he travelled the country, playing clubs, taverns, concerts, and concert houses. Through the years, he maintained his life on a meager income playing music, and doing odd jobs.

In 1977, he landed a cable T.V. show in Honolulu, Hawaii, called Music Session. Later that year, he decided to meet one of his brothers who was getting out of the Marines, and move to Oregon, where he continued music, and odd jobs, and studying metaphysical meditations. He lived in the foothills, along the McKenzie River, until the 1990s', when he purchased a home near the river.